Destination ardeN

By:

Dr. Nedra L. Johnson

I want to thank God for my talent.

Thank you, dear family and friends, for your inspiration.

A special thanks to my mom, Bobbie Johnson,
 my first teacher.

To Jimmy Lee, who TOLD me 13 years ago
to let my voice be HEARD.

I hope that these words bring you motivation and
encouragement.

                        Enjoy.

I Want to Learn You

What makes you smile?

What makes you wild?

My mind is open without fear.

What makes you shed that sincere tear?

What makes your happiness go away?

What makes up your agenda for a day?

What motivates you?

What makes you ache deep down inside?

What makes you put aside your pride?

What makes a goodnight's rest?

What causes you the most stress?

What's your favorite meal?

What do you do when you just want to chill?

I want to know you.

That's all I ask?

Notice, I asked nothing about your past.

I want to learn YOU

Thank You

Times have changed, and I have to question

If feelings are still the same

The things we did, we don't do anymore

It once was an adventure

That we both wanted to explore

I need a closed door

My heart is sore

The time has come for me to call it quits

I'm tired to the stories, lies,

 and the bullshit

I am a Queen and should be treated as such

Yes, I miss all of you

Including your touch

I have lied to myself for quite a while

Listening to your words

Being deceived by

Your style

I was into you and that I won't deny

I must grant you a strong farewell and goodbye

But before I depart

Know that you will always have a place in my heart

It's bad that there was so much going on

What we had for some reason is still

 unknown

So, thanks for the lesson, I have earned my 'A'

I can't promise another time

 nor day.

Everlasting You

I didn't know how much I missed you

Until I saw you last

Looking into your eyes

I saw memories of our past

Feeling the magic

Called us

With the laughs and hugs

My lover, my motivation

My number one fan

My best friend

When I met you it was a new feeling

Welcoming a journey unknown without an ending

It was love at first sight

As we hugged and said good night

I knew you would captivate my mind and

steal my heart

Everlasting you

You asked for my name, instead I gave you my soul

Right from the start

Autumn Moon

How lovely I perceive you as your presence dominates the sky.

Your image is captivating to my eye

As I glance at your magnificent glow

And how you pierce my soul

You perplex me with your diversity

I sometimes view fractions of you each image as powerful as your

whole

Your energy appears to emerge without a quest to monopolize your

space

You are opposites a common phrase

Some will speculate a fight

A struggle to be seen

You both share the same space

When daylight comes, it seems to capture your space

I know that you are there, I am remembering your grace

Even when my vision disputes

I still feel your presence, the presence of you

Caught UP

To some it's not an issue

No big deal

But I have a dilemma caused by these feelings that I feel

Contemplating thoughts of us

Trying extremely hard to trust

Part of me is blinded by a vision that I refuse to see

A voice shouting

Sometimes things are not meant to be

As I close my eyes and become intoxicated with remembrance of our time

When I open my eyes

 I have to question my thoughts consumed in my mind. Was I lost?

Some how did I get caught in the net, deceived by the bait

I can't control my thoughts every single day

And then your words, why do you say what you say?

To make me stronger

Really, they make the pain stay

Release this net and free my soul

Because at this moment I have lost control

Can We Talk?

I just want to talk to you

To know what's on your mind.

I want to get to know you and share a little of your time.

This is my request and invitation to engage

In one on one conversation, a beginning stage

I will be a respectful listener

My objective is to learn you

So, we can become occupied to adventures old and new

Let's intoxicate ourselves, with knowledge of each other

If it's meaningful we can extend further

I just want to talk to you

To know what's on your mind.

I want to get to know you and share a little of your time.

I Am

I am like

Water

Refreshing

Essential

With the power to destruct

Goals unquestionable

Desires unmeasurable

To those who can't comprehend

Premeditated Seduction?

One would question

The motive of Premeditated Seduction

The phone rings as I exit the shower

Are you ready? It's been minutes to an hour.

No, I have no clothes on. I am in the nude.

His response was," what else is new?"

Open the door.

I let him in….

Into our lover's den

I feel his eyes make footprints as I lead

He is

Undressing my skin

Reaching my soul

Without any help

I am his "Mocha" in a personified kind of way

He asked me what I wanted

I respond as I cut to the chase

You know what I want

Then his clothes were erased

Submerged bodies in oceans of lust

Increasing anticipation

Bodies in motion like tectonic plates

Points of subduction

He identifies as seduction

I say in a silent yet audible manner

My words not intended to be heard

But he savors every word

Like the touch of my body tight

Against his skin

He hears me say

That I have been

Contemplating this night all day

He says you seduced me, because you know the

Views of your still sand dunes…

 I like

Would you say that was Premeditated Seduction? Wrong, or Right?

A Morning Thought

The sun rises

Making us aware

A new day before us

God has granted another chance

To receive the gift of life

A new day and the question is

Will you be a blessing or a problem?

Leaves of Life

Without the power

To choose your desired tree

Or its location

Be realistic of

The fact that change will occur

Accept it and learn

There are times to stand tall

Times you may fall

But dance with the wind

Your environment influences your actions

Respond with reason

Natures elements

predetermined paths

at different seasons

Keep a pleasant tone

You never know who's listening

Or observing your phototropism

Appreciate the diversity

Each leaf so unique

Your colors evolve from Spring to Fall

Allow your leaves of life

To provide an example of beauty for all

Last Words

What did you do on your way out today?

Did you hug or look at a loved one and say…?

I love you, I love you with all my heart.

I will miss you dearly while we are apart.

Have a wonderful day.

Treat each day as if your last.

Never reflect on negative energies of the past.

Forget the mood, instead say

I love you I love you

Life is short, give every day your best.

Respect times for working, family, and times for rest.

Because.......

When bridges fall and then the call.

You think I should have given my all.

Flashbacks of those special times together

laughing, playing, or doing whatever

When?

The next day comes and you feel alone

Your loved one didn't make it home

The hurt, the pain and mostly regret

You stopped speaking just because you were upset.

That morning....

You walked out to start your day

So angry at small things that

You didn't want to say

I love you, I love you with all my heart.

I will miss you dearly while we are apart.

Have a wonderful day.

Let Time

The time is closely

Connected to the present

Influencing the future

Character flaws and talents

Will come full circle

Life would be much sweeter if while in the present

We let time respond to

All uncertainties

True experience is an instructional tool

But the method in which you use time

Grants peace of mind

That Polo Shirt

That Polo Shirt

Really turns me on

Wishing my hands were yours

As you tuck and untuck that

Polo Shirt

The variety of colors intrigue me

Leading to mysteries

I desire to discover

From plaids, stripes, long sleeves, short sleeves, Earth tones

To adventurous zones of color

I want to hug you in your Polo Shirt

I see you and I notice how the 100% cotton caresses your anatomy

I am not alone

There is a gravitational optic effect that others experience

I know that they are feeling you

Hell, I do too

But the difference is, just like That Polo Shirt is feeling you

You are feeling me, and I am not wearing That Polo Shirt

Yet

Decisions

Living a dream that I never dreamed

Unexplainable are these feelings

The once unknown have become my comfort zone

In these moments I have grown

The water level is high

Reflecting from the sky

Collecting thought after thought

Getting caught

Releasing issues and conflicts

Time matters

Erasing experience from the was

Numb to the past reality

The water has become a mirror

A reflection of growth

In the woman

That I have become

Understanding Self-Love

Has become a condition

No explanation

Required

Drivers Education 101

You feel it inside

So, you take a ride

Destination known

Yet unknown

Upon arrival all answers

To questions

have grown

into reality...................

Now what is your reaction?

No longer consumed with the chemistry and physical attraction

You want more but it's shared

Action Requested

Change your route-Too many roadblocks

Driving in hazardous conditions

Can lead to accidents-Calamity

No longer is a safety belt necessary

Full coverage is now

Void so relinquish the title and

License of your desire

-Drive Safely

SHERBET

When asked what do you think contributes to our bond?

His response was.......

You know how you live in a place and travel to another city

And in that city, you visit a shop that serves SHERBET

You experience a NEW and DIFFERENT taste

You love frozen desserts

But never tasted SHERBET

The first spoonful

So Delightful

So Amazing

Your taste buds become so demanding that you

Fall in love with SHERBET

You love Sherbet so much that you move to that city

Just meters away from the SHERBET shop

NOW you have the pleasure

Of having SHERBET

everyday

Every thought is about

SHERBET

But you don't want anyone to know that you

LOVE SHERBET

like Life

Until…...

One day you decide to try other cold desserts

Greed

Not the same pleasure as your

SHERBET

Months, Years, and Decades pass

You STILL desire your

SHERBET

And then one day you return to that shop

Surprisingly

It still serves

SHERBET

You order a bowl of SHERBET

And it STILL taste the same

You are my SHERBET

The Capacity to Love

You ask do I have the capacity to love?

A strong affection arising out of kinship or personal ties

More than a sexual embrace

More than a sexual episode

An object of warm affection of devotion

Interpersonal

Unrequited

Infatuation

Empty

Romantic

Companionate

Some say-

Release an emotional attachment that may be keeping you tied to the

past,

 break free and experience

 a feeling of instant healing

I say-

Love doesn't have legs to walk all over you

Love can tell time so it doesn't stay out all night

Love doesn't practice disrespect or betrayal

Love practices respect and loyalty

Love doesn't creep when it's deep

Love stays in the bed where it sleeps

So-

Do I have the capacity to love?

Well-

It's much easier to give love-unconditionally

        when

        the one

        you

        love

is doing right by demonstrating the capacity to love-

not the capacity to say LOVE

Andre

I thought about you today and couldn't help

But smile

I thought about you today and had to

Write it down

Do you remember picking berries and the

fun it would be?

What about going to 711, when we were afraid to cross the street?

Junior High and that "Candy Game"

Fights would break out in the school hallway, what a shame

Over Jolly Ranchers and Now and Later candy

Oh....

the longevity of the hallway makes me nauseous

Skyline Highschool was the place

Reading the dictionary was our race

As we grew older and became adults

Distance gradually separated us

Phone conversations for hours

Greeting sunrises

But distance will never change

Spoken Word

Simply just letters

Connected to form a word

Spitting promises I have frequently heard

A trusting tone

With a motive to do wrong

Words empty with meaning

Attacking my heart Bleeding

Bleeding

A bitter taste

Greeting your voice

Not guarding my heart

Trusting your spoken word

Water

If water could speak….What would it say?

Would it ask to wash all of your troubles away?

Or would it use a relaxing tone to ask about the events of your day?

Water caresses the body and mind

What if we are in the water at the same time?

Could water communicate how much I miss you?

It's real, because I feel you as the water

Touching every part of me

Each splash

Your voice

Water droplets

Your kiss

More than just H2O

A shower

Lasting an hour

The bath tub has transformed into my bed

Water is our silent source of communication

A soul connection

Enough said

Regret

In a dark room

No music no T.V.

All I have are memories

Memories of you with me

It feels like my eyes are closed

But they are wide open

Regret

My reflection in this dark room is like looking in the mirror

I see that US is no more because of me

You were a blessing

A treasure

Not perfect but perfect in reality

My dreams are now of you

Heart aching thru the night

When I share my thoughts

You assure me that I will be alright

I tell you that I am alone

You say be strong

Regret

Focus on those things that matter beyond this present time

Find you something to do that's productive for the mind

When the time is right

love will find you

But yet

Regret

It's difficult to focus

With thoughts of us

Missing everything

I wake up and go to sleep with tears

How could I be so stupid all those years?

Regret

You loved me with the greatest degree of unconditional love

You were patient with my mistakes

You stood by me with the heartaches

Regret

You gave our love a chance

All you ever wanted was love, respect, and romance

I had it all

My greed caused true love to fall

Apart

Now you have given me my space, freedom to move on

I still feel and want your toxic love

Am I wrong?

This regret is so strong.

If given the chance to do it

Again

Would be like

driving down a dead end

Regret

My Erotic Room

In my erotic room

I am your guide

To view my floor plan is by

Appointment and invitation only

As you enter my exotic place

Where aquatics co-exist with deserts

You will feel my ocean of sunshine

The utmost pleasure

You will view no pictures on my walls

But my walls do speak

And the sensation of conversation

Depends on the form, intent, and longevity of visitation

This room will give hospitality

Hugging while providing comfort

No crown molding or wall to wall

Carpet

The fireplace is always lit

Waiting for the right guest to extinguish it

The lawn has curb appeal

Manicured

A warm oasis awaits

Greeting by invitation only

And when you cum

I will love it

Even Though I don't have flood insurance

Freedom to Love

I remember falling in love with you

Like yesterday

Years passed

But not my love

I still get chills when you call my name

All day long I think of you, me, and us

Counting the minutes until our bodies touch

Life experiences have prepared me for you

And you for me

Someone familiar

But at the same time

New

A rebuilding of lost time

A rebuilding of us

A past imperfect

A past of hurt and pain

But it's ours

It is our bond

Definitely better than bad

It's not for others to understand

Apologies granted

Time heals

The connection still strong

You found me

And you are

Ready to give

our love a second chance

Unlike yesterday

No more secrets

To our romance

We can share our love

Without being judged

Freedom to love each other

After all of these years

Our love is a puzzle

We are now brave enough to

Leave the pieces on the table

For all to see

completed

There are many pieces to this puzzle

Very small pieces

The good part is that there are

No missing pieces

It's going to require time

I love you still

Always have and Always will

Just like yesterday

Time

Embrace the minute

The choices we make are valued or lost

No cost

Yet payment due

In due time

Sometimes we must hold our tongue

People never forget what we say

Purposeful actions

Behave is a meaningful way

So how important is this minute?

Minutes equal hours

Hours equal days

Days equal weeks

Weeks equal months

Months equal years

Years equal decades

Decades of smiles, sunshine

Storms and tears

Sixty seconds-so short and seems so small

Yet powerful enough to impact all

Voices

I am in so much pain

I can't believe that I am experiencing this

I just walked out mad

No words No kisses

Just angry and Frustrated

My life may be ending

In this hospital bed

My family and friends surround me

I can hear them

They can't hear me

I see their tears

I see the hurt in their faces

I wish we could be in a different place

They traveled great distances

Just to see me like this

Oh, wait the doctor just walked in

I am unconscious

I can't make sense of what he's saying

Then a voice speaks

Repeats

What did the doctor say?

The voice speaks something so encouraging

You can go home today

Broken Glass

Wake up you are a diamond

You are a woman with talent, intelligence, and class

Don't allow him to treat you like

Broken glass

Can't you see the magic number is three-strikes

Reflect on the time spent

The days of the nights

When the weekend comes, he has already come

Now kicking it with someone whom answers to a different name

How much longer will it take

For you to realize

That his only interest connects your thighs

You know what it is

But you are in a state of denial by his sight

Just caught up in the fictitious, sensual rhythms

That last all night

Wake up you are a diamond

You are a woman with talent, intelligence, and class

Don't allow him to treat you like

Broken glass

They say once tasted

You crave

Well you've tasted it, craved it, now grave it

He is a colossal waste of your time

So, when he calls

Love yourself enough not to cater to his will

It's Monday night he calls to say

'Hey baby, I have been missing you, I NEED to see you today."

Wake up you are a diamond

You are a woman with talent, intelligence, and class

Don't allow him to treat you like

Broken glass

You will feel weak because you know his loving is the bomb

Well the bomb just exploded

Slumber time has come to an end

The alarm is buzzing

Don't pretend

Please don't press snooze

If you continue to sleep

He will win again

And you will lose

Yourself

Wake up you are a diamond

You are a woman with talent, intelligence, and class

Don't allow him to treat you like

Broken glass

A New Emotion

I was never insecure until I met you

You made me do things that

I never thought I'd do

Like constant calls

And text after text

Unpredictable actions of what

I would do next

At one time I thought I was the shit

But your actions slowly caused me to forget

The way you cheated and way you lied

Constant heartbreak

As I cried and cried

Trying to figure out

What will it take to be your all?

Each time I stand

I'd fall into a place of a

Broken and Weak

Afraid to be alone

Afraid to choose

Peace and be Strong

Motivation

My dream your dream

May not be the same

But the common factor is

without effort

A dream is nothing but a name

You laugh at mine

It's so comical to you

It seems unreal

Something you think that I cannot do

Like the mighty wind blows

Down barriers

As it carries

Its weight

My dream may

Make you laugh but know

My dream you can't take

I dream big

And small ones too

Keep laughing cause

My dream one day will

Impact you

Like a wagon with a broken wheel

A dream is nothing

Until effort makes it real

There were many before me with such a quest

Dreams are more that dreams

When you strive for the best

Laughter will come with the journey of many test

Now you joke of this dream of mine

Keep laughing while

My efforts, my stride, my results

And in due time

You will recall this conversation of today

You will stop laughing

Become silent

Meditate and say

Laughter in response to a person's dream

Is really not as comical and unreal

As it may seem

Dream BIG

Favorites

This is what I feel………...

You are my light that shines through a dark passage.

You are my glass of water on a hot summer day.

You are my pillow when I'm sleepy.

You are my cover when I'm cold.

My all-time FAVORITE.

My favorite movie

My favorite food

My favorite color

My favorite mood

You are my favorite purse that I carry, when I wear my favorite outfit.

You are my sunshine on a cloudy day.

You are my umbrella in stormy weather.

You are my favorite song to sing.

My all-time FAVORITE.

My favorite drink

My favorite book

My favorite taste

My favorite look

You are my favorite birthday present.

You are my favorite dessert.

You are my favorite amusement park ride.

You are my favorite dance.

My favorite touch

My favorite pain

My favorite misunderstanding

My favorite name

My favorite thought

My all-time FAVORITE.

This is what I know.........

Reality is that sometimes our favorites can be the most destructive.

It's because of our favorites, that we are easily influenced.

Favorites create the release of indiscretions.

Having no limits-No premeditations

Caught up with the favorites, that self-image is lost.

Priorities become scattered

Headed for self-destruction and it doesn't matter

Yet we still love our favorites, even with a broken heart.

This is what I know.

Thoughts

I reminisce on our past encounters the good and the bad

Wondering if your feelings are still

Or are they feelings you had

I can't help to have constant thoughts of you

Questioning daily, what are you up to?

Now I understand

The man

The woman I have become

Worshiping the idea of a relationship

From day one

I should have known better

When I chose us

Instead of me

Reality

A strong woman

Lost in an image for others to see

Letting go and moving on a forced action

You did it first

Your actions made me let go

Yet I thirst

For a lie

When you show me the truth…

Each time you come by

Why?

I remain strong

And enjoy this peace of mind

What we had was a place, moment in time

A bond unbroken

Words unspoken

Nothing matters at this point

Just a point of no return

A major and lasting

lesson learned

He Said

He said that no one told him how to be a husband

He said that no one showed him how to be a man

A commitment

He said that he didn't fully understand

He said that he didn't know how to love

Because he didn't love himself

He said that no one showed him how to be a role model

When he reached for

the bottle

An escape

He said that he didn't fully internalize

The abuse reflected in a loved one eyes

Because he didn't love himself

He said that it's a struggle being who he is

He said that he's constantly being judged by his peers

Internal conflict

A constant fight

Seems like 24 hours of the darkest night

He said that

An Experience

After all these years, I wondered what life was bringing him

How were his days and nights?

I never thought that he would be the one to bring me a storm

Cold blooded a man without a conscience

I gave all of the love I had to give

Giving every part of me

Sometimes I felt that I didn't have all of him

No guards no limitations I accepted him

Hoping with each passing day

Things would get better

Not knowing that I would transform into a floor

I allowed him to walk and stomp on my heart

In certain situations

There is no need for communication

When it's understood

It took me to experience heartbreak to see the reality

Actions and behaviors reflect character and personality

Loving with loyalty, honesty, and commitment

Does not produce intentional pain to your love one

He was my first love and I wanted him to be

My last kiss

My last love

Forever Us

WRONG

My life was like a movie without commercials

Some thought that I was going crazy

Wanting him more than anything in life

Wanting him more than life

Then those words

Knowing that I you love me is all that matters

Practicing self-isolation to conceal the truth

The hurt and disrespect

Matter forming so intense that only a shower

Camouflages the tears but not the pain

DENIAL

Shown the glass of water, but I wanted to see otherwise

Imagining a refreshing beverage

Analyzing the difference between the crushed and blocked ice

Adding lemons to sanitize

Our love was a glass of water

I gave you clean and clear

I thought and wanted to believe

Instead you allowed the ground to consume my water

ACCEPTANCE

I allowed you to treat me like a finished cigarette

Thank you for letting me see

That for a moment, I forgot about me

I gave you my love and my trust you stole

REALITY

I silently gave you the permission to be you.

Have You Ever?

Have you ever wanted someone so bad?

That

everything that you do, see, taste, smell, and touch

consumes thoughts of that person.

Imaging that every object that you touch is that person's hand

Have you ever tossed and turned all night?

Thinking about that person

Have you ever experienced that each time you close your eyes, you see that person?

Have you ever felt that letting go was not an option?

Letting go should be an option

Have you ever felt a love so deep and real, yet complicated?

Have you ever been thinking of that person then the phone rings and it's them?

Have you ever experienced a broken yet an unbroken bond with someone?

Have you ever had a broken heart and still loved that person just the same, if not more?

Have you ever experienced unconditional love?

Have you ever wanted things to be better, but knew it would be unrealistic?

Have you ever tried to stop thinking about that person for just one day and it never happens?

Intuition

She asks the question

Because she really wants to know

Know not the truth, because it is a lie

Anticipating your response

She knows the answer

Listening to you go on and on

Adding fabrications to the truth

Hurting her absolutely not

This is an intoxicating pleasure

More enjoying than her favorite shot

And you say that your game is 'TIGHT"

Checkmate, game point, fourth quarter no over time

Bottom of the ninth

All bases loaded, she steps to the base

"Grand Slam"

The M.V.P.

The V.I.P. in L.I.F.E.

If you knew

You would shut up

She says that society influences the liar

And the liar manipulates

To gaslight and cover secrets and betrayal

She said that she can influence us

If we just take the time to listen

To a tone

Having a volume so low, yet powerfully loud

Intercepting hard ache, pain, and above all

"Wasted Time"

She said acknowledge me

Let me guide you and you will

laugh more instead of crying

A Different Tone

Have you ever had that person you love tell you that you didn't love

yourself?

Because if you did

You would exit the relationship…….

I've gathered the broken pieces

And yes, I have moved on

Years ago, I was weak

But currently I am strong

I have tried to write on the topic

Of lies, deceit, and pain

But right now, it's somewhat difficult

Since those feelings don't remain

Remembering how I grown from the pain

Now I indulge in the beautiful me

Reflecting no longer on what should have been

Acknowledging that what we had

Has reached a dead end

Experiencing a drama free

Tranquil lifestyle

Being in love with my own style

Loving my touch

And the sound of my voice

Always choosing me

As my primary choice

Accepting and learning from

My mistakes of the past

Indulging in this love called SELF

That I know will Everlast

From my intimate conversations

To the self-gratifications

While practicing self-modification

I am in love with ME

No insecurity

No jealousy

An unconditional love

2020 Hope

The Sun speaks each morning

conversations with the trees

the rays from this voice encourages me

to listen to the trees

acknowledging their diversity

while respecting

natures touch

as the leaves

allow the season to be

the blueprint of change

they too have conversations

of hope

teaching me that

some things are beyond our control

and we have to appreciate life itself

having hope

standing in the midst of

chaos and uncertainty

knowing that even though

their leaves change

knowing that even though

their leaves may fall

yet for some

not to be envious of the

Evergreen

Everything

 is a

SEASON

A SEASON of HOPE

The trees understand that the SUN is their ENERGY

The Photosynthesis of hope

The trees are our OXYGEN

We NEED TO Breathe

I know that it's HARD

We are motivated by the TREES

Look to the trees

A Voice of HOPE